Ellandar Productions and Theatre503 present

NO
PARTICULAR
ORDER

by **Joel Tan** 陈文传

No Particular Order was first produced in an amateur production by the Oxford School of Drama at Southwark Playhouse, London, on 21 July 2021, and first produced in a professional production by Ellandar Productions and Theatre503 at Theatre503, London, on 31 May 2022.

NO PARTICULAR ORDER

by **Joel Tan** 陈文传

Cast	Jules Chan
	Pandora Colin
	Pía Laborde-Noguez
	Daniel York Loh
Director	Joshua Roche
Designer	Ingrid Hu
Lighting Designer	Clare O'Donoghue
Sound Designer & Composer	Sarah Sayeed
Video Designer	Erin Guan and Isabel Sun of Vroom Lab Theatre
Producer	Iskandar إسكندر R. bin Sharazuddin
Producer	Mingyu Lin 林铭宇
Production Manager	Patricia Gilvaia
Stage Manager	Rose Hockaday

Jules Chan

Jules graduated from Drama Centre London and has since worked at the National Theatre (2020), Southbank Centre (2020) and at the end of 2021 he wrote, directed and performed in his own play *Days in Quarantine*. He is the co-founder of Rising Waves – a mentorship programme for British East and South East Asians supported by Arts Council England. In 2022 he has been working extensively with movement based company The Pappy Show on their new production called *What Do You See?* (2022) at The Shoreditch Town Hall, and most recently on their hit show *BOYS* (2022) at the Barbican – for the theatre's fortieth-year anniversary.

Pandora Colin

Pandora has a large number of screen credits, and is best known for her roles in HBO miniseries *Chernobyl*, Netflix's *Master of None*, *Black Books*, *Delicious*, *Line of Duty*, and *Count Arthur Strong*. Films include Nicholas Hytner's *The Lady in the Van*, *Earwig and the Witch* (Studio Ghibli), and *I Give It A Year*.

Most recent theatre credits include *Bach & Sons* (Bridge Theatre); *8 Hotels* (Minerva, Chichester Festival Theatre); *Our Town* (Regent's Park Open Air Theatre); *A Midsummer Night's Dream* (Sheffield Crucible); *The Vote* (Donmar Warehouse); *House of Bernarda Alba*, *The Dark Earth and the Light Sky* (Almeida Theatre); *Women of Troy*, *Some Trace of Her*, *Every Good Boy* and *After the Dance* (National Theatre).

Pía Laborde-Noguez

Pía graduated with a BA in Acting from the Royal Academy of Dramatic Art. She's half French, half Mexican. Theatre includes *A Fight Against...* (Royal Court); *The House of the Spirits*, *The House of Bernarda Alba* (Cervantes); *Una niña es una cosa a medio formar* (Sala Beckett & Museo Tamayo); *Trust* (Gate Theatre); *Glorious!* (Frinton Festival); *The Tempest* (Norwich & Norfolk Theatre Festival); *Boat* (Pigdog); *Current Location*, *Five Days in March* (Fellswoop); *The Seagull* (Célébration 43).

Television includes *Todo va a estar bien*, *Mallorca Files, Nina & The Pig*. Film includes: *Volcanes*, *Control*, *Tilda & Laila* [short], *Los Paisajes, La Cocina*.

Daniel York Loh 丹尼约克罗

Theatre includes the Royal Shakespeare Company, National Theatre, Donmar Warehouse, Royal Court, Hampstead Theatre, Finborough, Gate, Edinburgh Traverse, Nuffield Southampton and most recently the European tour of *LOVE* by Alexander Zeldin (Odéon-Théatre de l'Europe) and *Dr. Semmelweis* (Bristol Old Vic). He has worked extensively in Singapore and in the feature films *The Beach*, *Scarborough*, *The Receptionist* as well as the award-winning web series, *Jade Dragon.*

As a writer his plays include *The Fu Manchu Complex* (Ovalhouse) and *Forgotten* 遗忘 (Arcola/Plymouth Theatre Royal). He is one of 21 'writers of colour' featured in the best-selling, award-winning essay collection *The Good Immigrant*. He is a founder member of Moongate Productions and associate artistic director of Chinese Arts Now with which he co-created and performed in *Every Dollar is a Soldier/With Money You're a Dragon* part of CAN x Two Temple Place which recently won the Arts Council Digital Culture Award (Storytelling). He has directed several short films incluing the award-winning *Hall of Mirrors* and *Laid* for RADA. He is one-third of alt-folk trio Wondermare whose self-titled album is available on Spotify, etc.

Joel Tan 陈文传 || **Playwright**

Joel Tan is a Singaporean playwright based between London and Singapore. His play *Love in the Time of the Ancients* was a finalist for the 2019 Papatango Prize, and *No Particular Order* was shortlisted for Theatre503's 2018 Playwriting Award. Joel was one of the 503Five resident playwrights at Theatre503 and was part of the 2020-2021 Royal Court Writers Group.

Recent work in the UK includes *When The Daffodils* (Orange Tree Theatre); *Living Newspaper* (Royal Court Theatre); *Overheard*, *Augmented Chinatown* (Chinese Arts Now). He has plays in development with Almeida Theatre, the Royal Court, and Headlong Theatre. Joel also works inter-disciplinarily, and has collaborated with visual artists, poets, musicians and dancers as a writer, director and dramaturg.

In Singapore, his plays have been produced by leading theatre companies including Checkpoint Theatre, Wild Rice, and Pangdemonium, and several are available in a collection, *Joel Tan Plays Volume 1*, published by Checkpoint Theatre.

Joshua Roche || Director

Josh Roche was the twentieth winner of the JMK Award for his production of *My Name is Rachel Corrie* at the Young Vic with Erin Doherty in the title role in 2017 ('Brilliant staging' – *WhatsOnStage*). Other work has included the first adaptation of George Saunders' work in the UK, *Winky* (Soho Theatre); Audible's first stage production in the UK – *Radio* by Al Smith; and first productions of new plays such as *Orlando* by Lucy Roslyn with Boondog and Jessie Anand, and *Plastic* by Kenny Emson at the Old Red Lion with Poleroid Theatre. For the RSC he directed *The Hamlet Sketch* in the BAFTA-nominated *Shakespeare Live!* with Judi Dench, Benedict Cumberbatch, Harriet Walter, Ian McKellen, Tim Minchin and others. He also directed the multi-lingual opening ceremony of The World Shakespeare Conference in 2016. Most recently he directed a major revival of David Storey's *Home* at Chichester Festival Theatre ('Captivating revival', four stars – *Guardian*). He is the co-founder of the OpenHire campaign for transparent hiring.

Ingrid Hu 胡嘉倩 || Designer

Ingrid Hu is an award-winning scenographer, designer, and artist working in theatre and multidisciplinary design in the UK and internationally. With a focus on materiality, contextual and conceptual thinking, she creates spaces and environments that are alive and empowered to co-author, investigate, and respond to varied perspectives. Recent credits include *Chotto Xenos* (Akram Khan, world tour); *The Global Playground* (MIF, Theatre Rites); *Athena, A Kettle of Fish* (The Yard Theatre, London, UK); *A Slightly Annoying Elephant* (Little Angel Theatre, London, UK); *Light/Dark* (Uppsala, Sweden); *Curioser* (UK/Norway tour), *Zeraffa Geraffa* (Little Angel Theatre, Clapham Omnibus Theatre, London, UK), *We Raise Our Hand in the Sanctuary* (The Albany, London, UK), *Hong Kong Impressions* (Yuen Long Theatre, Hong Kong); *1908: Body and Soul* (Jacksons Lane Theatre, London, UK) and *You May!* (The Place, Arnolfini, UK, Onassis Culture Centre, Greece) among others. Awards include 2014 Aesthetica Art Prize finalist (3D design & sculpture), 2011 D&AD Yellow Pencil award (UK Pavilion, Heatherwick Studio), 1998 Neptune Theatre Blackmore Award, Canada, 1996 Caran d'Arche Sunday Artist of the Year, Hong Kong.

Clare O'Donoghue || Lighting Designer

After studying German and Drama at Goldsmiths College,

University of London, Clare worked in lighting in various theatres including Sadler's Wells and the National Theatre, finally as Deputy Lighting Manager of Glyndebourne Festival Opera. After assisting renowned lighting designer Jennifer Tipton, Clare managed her own design with reviving operas and dance shows around the world for companies including the Royal Opera House, National Theatre and Deutsche Oper Berlin. She has combined design with working as a freelance production engineer, making and installing lighting effects for international shows and events.

Lighting Design includes *Bird*, *Manchild* (Amina Khayyam Dance Company); *Helter Skelter* (Cockpit Theatre); *Freud's Last Session* (Nearly There Productions); *Blu and the Magic Web* (Truestory Theatre); *Dido and Aeneas* (Royal Academy of Music); *Frankenstein*, *Great Expectations* (National Youth Theatre); *The Marriage of Figaro*, *Don Giovanni* (Glyndebourne Touring Opera); *One Snowy Night* (Seabright Productions); *Slideshow* (Slot Machine); *Down by the Greenwood Side* (Brighton Festival); *Eat This/Drink That*, *The Finnish Prisoner*, *The Young Visitors* (The Paddock); *Ghatam* (ATMA Dance); *Guys and Dolls* (Central School of Speech and Drama); *Tycho's Dream*, *Into The Harbour*, *Lovers Walk* (Glyndebourne Youth Opera); *The New World Order* (Hydrocracker/Brighton Festival); *So Close To Home* (Mapp Productions, Arcola Theatre, Brighton Festival); *The Fairy Queen* (Brighton Early Music Festival); *Here's What I Did With My Body One Day* (Lightworks).

Sarah Sayeed || Sound Designer & Composer

Sarah Sayeed is a musician, composer, sound designer and writer with over fifteen years of experience working collaboratively with a range of artists and on productions.

As a musical artist, her practice focuses around contemporary works that are influenced by a plethora of styles and musical traditions. Sarah has created compositions and sound designs across Western classical choral works, Indian and Bengali classical vocals, instrumental pieces and her first love: contemporary jazz, soul and hip hop. Sarah plays instruments tanpura and shruti, and is the lead vocalist in international duet Myth of Her with violin and electronic artist Anne Eltard (Copenhagen, Denmark). Sarah is currently training in classical vocals with leading Classical Indian Music maestro Swati Natekar and was the successful recipient of the Portfolio Composers Scheme in partnership with Sound and Music and Kuljit Bhamra.

Sarah's credits include Composer and Sound Designer for
Santi and Naz (The Thelmas); Composer and Sound Designer
for *We Are Shadows* (Tamasha); Principal Musician in *Richard II*
(Shakespeare's Globe 2019); Composer and Musical Director for
the Royal Shakespeare Company adaption of Molière's *Tartuffe*
(2019/2018) and Sound Designer for Contact Theatre's production
on Suffragette Movement, *She Bangs the Drums* (2018). In 2021
she worked on *10 Nights* directed by Kash Arshad (co-production
with Graeae and Tamasha at the Bush Theatre) and Shakespeare's
in Italy *A Merchant of Venice*, directed by Bill Alexander. Sarah has
recently finished her first major dance score *Alexa Stop* for SAA-UK
(South Asian Arts) and is currently working on *Born and Bread* with
Brighton People's Theatre.

Erin Guan 关绰莹 || Video Designer

Erin is a London-based set and costume designer and interactive
installation designer from China, a graduate of Royal Central
School of Speech and Drama and UCL. She has a strong interest
in interdisciplinary theatre and performance making and she
works across installations, plays, musicals, dance, digital theatre,
and devised theatre. Erin's work spans across intercultural
performances and minority voices. Her digital artwork specialises
in digital art Augmented Reality and Virtual Reality experiences.
Her VR installation *Chamber404* exhibited with Ars Electronica 2020
and Interactive Architecture Lab, Camden People's Theatre and
VAULT Festival 2022.

Recent theatre projects include immersive technology promenade
performance *Unchain Me* (Dreamthinkspeak & Brighton Festival);
Symbiont (Caged Bird Theatre & The Vault); *Foxes* (Defibrillator
Theatre & Theatre503); touring musical *Tokyo Rose* (Burnt Lemon
Theatre); immersive game theatre *Talk* and *The House Never Wins*
(Kill The Cat Theatre); *Freedom Hi* 自由閪, *Asian Pirate Musical*
(PaperGang Theatre); devising interactive performance *Money
Funny Sunny* (Cheeky Chin TC). Erin also worked as an assistant
designer to *Faces in the Crowd* (Gate Theatre); *Does My Bomb Look
Big in This?* (Soho Theatre); and *Summer Rolls* (Park Theatre).

Isabel Sun 孫瑀 || Video Designer

Isabel Sun was born in Taiwan and attended UCL, receiving a
MArch in Design for Performance and Interaction in 2021. Her
body of work ranges from collaborative performances with the

modern dance group Happy Cola's Friends (2020-2022) to self-directed VR plays such as *Chamber404* (2021). She has three years experience in creating animation and operating the projection and LED visual for concerts, commercial shows and theatre.

Iskandar إسكندر R. bin Sharazuddin || Producer

Iskandar is an award-winning British-Bruneian playwright and theatre-maker, the Co-Founder, Producer and Joint Artistic Director of Ellandar Productions. He is the Communities Associate at Headlong Theatre Ltd., and currently teaches at Guildhall School of Music and Drama and Arts Educational Schools London.

As producer for Ellandar Productions theatre credits include *Finding Melania* (Underbelly, Edinburgh Fringe 2022 and Camden People's Theatre SPRINT Festival 2021); *At Broken Bridge* (Camden People's Theatre 2022); *[The Cobbled Streets of Geneva]* (VAULT Festival 2020, Winner: Origins Award for Outstanding New Work Theatre & Performance); *Post-Mortem* (Edinburgh Fringe 2019, The Blue Room Theatre & Fringe World Festival Western Australia 2020, and Holden Street Theatres, Adelaide Fringe 2020); *(un)written (un)heard* (Fringe World Festival Western Australia 2020, Winner: International Dance & Physical Theatre Award); *Silently Hoping* (VAULT Festival 2019 & Applecart Arts).

Other selected theatre credits include Movement Director on *Cosí fan tutte* and Deputy Movement Director on *Satyagraha* (English National Opera 2021/22); Associate Movement Director on *The Climbers* (Theatre by the Lake). He is the recipient of the 2014 Tony Craze Playwriting Award for his play *The Life of Cardboard*.

Mingyu Lin 林铭宇 || Joint Artistic Director of Ellandar

Ming is a director for stage and screen, she's a Creative Associate at Headlong, a Resident Artist with York Theatre Royal and a Reader for Traverse Theatre and the Bruntwood Prize. She's a recipient of Living Pictures' Directors' bursary 2021 and a founding member of BESEA advocacy group BEATS. Ming trained at the Royal Central School of Speech and Drama and is an alumna of the Royal Court Writers' Programme.

As a screen director she directs for *Hollyoaks* (Channel 4) and has won finalist awards for *Sundance Shorts*, *Sci-Fi London*, *Enter the Pitch* and ITN's *Nativity Factor*.

As an audio director she has directed *Out Of The Woods* (Tamasha) and *Waiting For A Chance To Turn* (Futures Theatre), which was nominated for a Women's Podcast Award and won a Silver Anthem Award.

As a stage director and dramaturg she has directed the Offie-nominated *Does My Bomb Look Big in This?* (Soho Theatre) and was dramaturg on Headlong's *Corrina, Corrina* (Liverpool Everyman Theatre). Selected stage directing credits include *Overheard* (York Theatre Royal/Notthingham Lakeside); *Babel* (ArtsEd); *Lòng Mẹ* (VAULT Festival 2020); *Silently Hoping* (Arcola Theatre, VAULT Festival, and Applecart Arts) and *No Bond So Strong* (MAC Birmingham).

Production Acknowledgements

Key Art Photography	Eivind Hansen
Art Direction	Louise Richardson
Rehearsal Photography and Video	Morgan Sinclair
Press Representation	Diana Whitehead of Fourth Wall PR

Many thanks to the cast of *No Particular Order* from the Oxford School of Drama at Southwark Playhouse: Oscar Adams, Callum Cronin, Ardan Devine, Abigail Mahony, Bethany Merryn, Jasmin Pitt, Christopher Watson.

And to the creative team at Southwark Playhouse: Emily Bestow (Designer), Alex Fernandes (Lighting Designer), Rachael Murray (Sound Designer), Mishi Bekesi (Production Manager).

This production was made possible with support from National Arts Council Singapore; Megan Iona Kirk; Chinese Arts Now; and Centre151.

ELLANDAR
PRODUCTIONS

Ellandar Productions || Producer & General Management

Ellandar are an award-winning and BESEA (British East & Southeast Asian) led London-based multidisciplinary theatre company.

Ellandar's work is narrative-focused and inclusive in form and content. They produce work platforming diverse British Muslim narratives, BESEA lived experiences, and women-led work. Originally founded by Elliott Cook and Iskandar إسكندر R. bin Sharazudin in Perth Western Australia, Ellandar have always been ambitious and diverse. They produce and commission work to challenge pervasive stereotypes, draw upon and celebrate difference, and bring characters and stories that are deeply human and recognisable centre stage.

Joint Artistic Director	Iskandar إسكندر R. bin Sharazuddin
Joint Artistic Director	Mingyu Lin 林铭宇
Assistant Producer	Cher Nicolette Ho 何彩彤
Assistant Producer	Himanshu Ojha

Theatre503 is at the forefront of identifying and nurturing new voices at the very start of their careers and launching them into the industry. They stage more early career playwrights than any other theatre in the world – with over 120 writers premiered each year from festivals of short pieces to full length productions, resulting in employment for over 1,000 freelance artists through their year-round programme. Theatre503 provides a diverse pipeline of talent resulting in modern classics like *The Mountaintop* by Katori Hall and *Rotterdam* by Jon Brittain – both Olivier Award winners – to future classics like Yasmin Joseph's *J'Ouvert*, winner of the 2020 James Tait Black Prize and transferred to the West End/BBC Arts and *Wolfie* by Ross Willis, winner of the 2020 Writers' Guild Award for Best New Play. Writers who began their creative life at Theatre503 are now writing for the likes of *The Crown*, *Succession*, *Doctor Who*, *Killing Eve* and *Normal People* and every single major subsidised theatre in the country now boasts a new play by a writer who started at Theatre503.

Theatre503 Team

Artistic Director	Lisa Spirling
Executive Director	Andrew Shepherd
Literary Manager	Steve Harper
Producer	Ceri Lothian
General Manager	Tash Berg
Carne Associate Director	Jade Lewis
Literary Associate	Lauretta Barrow
Technical Manager	Toby Smith
Trainee Assistant Producers	Hadeel Elshak
	Myles Sinclair
Marketing Officer	Millie Whittam
Administrator	Lizzie Akita
Associate Company	45North

NO PARTICULAR ORDER

Joel Tan

Characters

Every scene starts afresh.

At least four actors – two young, two older, a mix of races and genders – play all the roles.

Notes

Thirty years separate *Part One* and *Part Two*.
Three hundred years separate *Part Two* and *Part Three*.

Notes on the Dialogue

A dash (–) at the end of a line indicates an interruption from the next speaker.

An ellipsis (…) at the end of the line indicates a trailing-off of the sentence.

A slash (/) indicates overlapping dialogue.

Lines that end without a full stop are unfinished thoughts.

This text went to press before the end of rehearsals and so may differ slightly from the play as performed.

PART ONE

1. Street

A despot has come to power.

Evening. Birds roosting for the night in the trees along a shopping street in an urban centre. It's a thunderous murmuration – a great noise of chirruping, flapping, rustling. EXTERMINATOR 1 *and* EXTERMINATOR 2 *are eating sandwiches.*

EXTERMINATOR 1. Careful you don't have bird shit in that.

EXTERMINATOR 2. They don't shit when they're like that.

EXTERMINATOR 1. Really?

EXTERMINATOR 2. Seen it enough times. Do you shit when you're going to bed?

EXTERMINATOR 1. I shit before.

EXTERMINATOR 2. But not when you're *going* to bed.

EXTERMINATOR 1. Sometimes. Do birds pee?

EXTERMINATOR 2. The water comes out in the shit, doesn't it? What've you got there?

EXTERMINATOR 1. Ham sandwich.

EXTERMINATOR 2. Nice. I have tuna. Trade one?

They swap their second sandwiches.

EXTERMINATOR 1. Noisy.

EXTERMINATOR 2. You'll get used to it.

EXTERMINATOR 1. Funny they still come here. Even with all these buildings. And in this part of town, too. Nice real estate, isn't it, for a bird?

EXTERMINATOR 2. Used to be a forest here, before they built the roads through. These trees are old, which is why it's such a pain, can't cut down the trees, but these damned birds. They like old trees. Gives them more room.

EXTERMINATOR 1. Like a chirping storm cloud isn't it? Kind of frightening. Can see why it gets to some people. Kind of beautiful, really.

EXTERMINATOR 2. How's that sandwich?

EXTERMINATOR 1. Good.

Enter BUREAUCRAT.

BUREAUCRAT. Good, you're here. Finish up, get started soon.

EXTERMINATOR 2. You're

BUREAUCRAT. From P&E.

EXTERMINATOR 1 (*to* Exterminator 2). P&E?

EXTERMINATOR 2. Parks and Environment.

BUREAUCRAT. Who's the boss?

EXTERMINATOR 2. I am. Here's the invoice.

BUREAUCRAT. We'll do that after.

EXTERMINATOR 2. Why?

BUREAUCRAT. Well. The last company we used didn't get the job done. Clearly.

EXTERMINATOR 2. No?

BUREAUCRAT. You can't hear them?

EXTERMINATOR 2. What?

BUREAUCRAT. The birds.

EXTERMINATOR 2. 'Course I can.

BUREAUCRAT. Then?

EXTERMINATOR 2. Right. Sorry.

BUREAUCRAT. So when can you get started?

EXTERMINATOR 2. Now.

BUREAUCRAT. Is it going to leave a mess? If it does you have to clean it, we don't have time for my people to

EXTERMINATOR 2. No, no, no, not if we do one tree at a time. We net them, you see, and –

BUREAUCRAT. A tree at a time?

EXTERMINATOR 2. Not a one day job.

BUREAUCRAT. Oh, you're not fucking serious. How long?

EXTERMINATOR 2. Didn't...

BUREAUCRAT. That's not what we asked for. We need them gone before – did you say nets? Don't you use that new thing, that, that, thing with the sound waves and the

EXTERMINATOR 2. The machine. *That* would leave a mess, you see, because they drop like flies.

EXTERMINATOR 1. Dead?

EXTERMINATOR 2. Dead.

EXTERMINATOR 1. Didn't know that. Wouldn't have had a sandwich before.

EXTERMINATOR 2. Well, except we weren't going to use that thing.

BUREAUCRAT. No, you are. I was told this would be done in a day.

EXTERMINATOR 2. By...

BUREAUCRAT. I don't care. I told my boss it'd be done in a day.

EXTERMINATOR 2. Why the rush?

BUREAUCRAT. You're not serious.

EXTERMINATOR 2. No.

BUREAUCRAT. The parade.

EXTERMINATOR 2. The

EXTERMINATOR 1. Oh yeah, that.

EXTERMINATOR 2. That, what?

EXTERMINATOR 1. They've got that victory parade coming through, what is it, day after tomorrow? Tanks and floats and all that.

BUREAUCRAT (*to* EXTERMINATOR 2). Why're you the boss?

EXTERMINATOR 2. Well, alright, there's two of us, with the nets we can do maybe two trees at a time. With the nets it's easy, you catch them live, put the birds in the truck, move on to the…

BUREAUCRAT. Okay, then call more people. It's not difficult.

EXTERMINATOR 2. It's a Saturday.

BUREAUCRAT. It's a Saturday. For fuck's sake. Look, the only reason we hired you is because this is supposed to –

EXTERMINATOR 2. It's the fastest way.

BUREAUCRAT. Well no, the machine stuns them dead, shoots them out of the sky in big black patches, doesn't it? With sounds waves. Right?

Fast. Instant.

EXTERMINATOR 2. We try not to kill them, you see, there's no need.

BUREAUCRAT. Did you bring it?

EXTERMINATOR 2.…

EXTERMINATOR 1. We did.

BUREAUCRAT. Simple. Will it cost more?

EXTERMINATOR 2. I'd really prefer if we stuck to the… it's a simple enough job, really, we can get it done by tomorrow if we… (*To* EXTERMINATOR 1.) If we worked fast and smart, I reckon, would net easily thirty of them at a go, looks to be about a thousand here?

EXTERMINATOR 1. I've got dinner at home.

EXTERMINATOR 2. Dinner

EXTERMINATOR 1. My wife's mother is cooking.

BUREAUCRAT. Look do you want me to lose my job?

EXTERMINATOR 2. Of course not.

BUREAUCRAT. 'Cuz I will. I fucking will lose my job if these birds are here fucking about during the parade. More than my job.

EXTERMINATOR 2. But they've always been here, you must've known that. We've tried to sort them out for years, but there's too many. They keep coming back.

BUREAUCRAT. He made promises. You heard him. About taking care of these kind of things.

Cleaning up the city. You tell me how to explain to my boss that on a live broadcast going out to the entire world, there's a black cloud of birds swooping about shitting on his parade, that we were supposed to have taken care of.

EXTERMINATOR 2. There'll be dead birds all over the street. Look, get someone else. We don't kill them if we don't have to.

BUREAUCRAT. Get someone else?

EXTERMINATOR 2. Get someone else.

BUREAUCRAT. I have people I could call.

EXTERMINATOR 2. Good.

BUREAUCRAT. You misunderstand.

EXTERMINATOR 2. What?

BUREAUCRAT. I said you misunderstand.

Silence.

EXTERMINATOR 1. We don't want any trouble.

BUREAUCRAT. Well.

Silence.

EXTERMINATOR 1 (*to* EXTERMINATOR 2). Hey. I'll go get it.

EXTERMINATOR 2....

EXTERMINATOR 1. Alright?

EXTERMINATOR 2....

EXTERMINATOR 1. Don't be such an asshole.

EXTERMINATOR 2....

EXTERMINATOR 1. I've got dinner.

EXTERMINATOR 2....

EXTERMINATOR 1. And you know how it is.

EXTERMINATOR 1 *exits.*

BUREAUCRAT. Good hire.

Silence.

Where's that invoice? Can I have a look at it?

EXTERMINATOR 2 *hands* BUREAUCRAT *the invoice.* BUREAUCRAT *scans it.*

I'll throw in some extra. For the cleanup.

EXTERMINATOR 1 *enters with a large metal box.*

That it?

EXTERMINATOR 1 *opens the box, inside is a device of some sort.*

BUREAUCRAT *whistles.*

Can I stay? To watch?

EXTERMINATOR 1 *takes out the device, positions it, pointing upwards.*

(*To* EXTERMINATOR 2.) You doing it?

EXTERMINATOR 1 *connects the device to an adaptor. Switches it on. A sound.*

It's on.

EXTERMINATOR 1 *steps away from the device.*

Pause.

EXTERMINATOR 2 *moves to the device.*

EXTERMINATOR 1 *hands around large mufflers. They all put them on.*

Expertly, EXTERMINATOR 2 *maneuvers the device. Takes aim. Releases a pulse of sound. A cascade of feathers.* EXTERMINATOR 2 *releases another. More feathers. Another pulse, more feathers.*

2. Backyard

WRITER 2 *and* WRITER 1 *are sitting at a table watching a distressing video, or listening to a live broadcast, on a device. It is of a man giving a speech, muffled. Midway,* WRITER 2 *turns it off and starts rolling a cigarette.*

WRITER 1. The last time we were here. That was nice, wasn't it?

WRITER 2. Frigid, far as I recall.

WRITER 1. We read pages from that –

WRITER 2. Frigid and wet.

WRITER 1. That novel of yours. Out here. My boyfriend made cake. Remember?

WRITER 2. My leather jacket got moldy from the rain.

WRITER 1. Whatever happened to that novel?

WRITER 2. I was sick for days.

WRITER 1. It wasn't that wet. No. It can't have been if we were out here.

WRITER 1 *starts up the broadcast again. After a moment:*

Whatever happened to those pages?

Pause.

WRITER 2. Tried turning them into a short story.

WRITER 1. Pity. I thought they were fantastic. / There was a...

WRITER 2. Didn't even finish that / short story.

WRITER 1. A kind of, I want to say heraldic... Heraldic quality. You know what I mean? Pointing to the future. A radical future. Angry verses from the future.

WRITER 2. I thought they were shit.

WRITER 1. Those were different times. Last year was different times.

WRITER 2. Well.

WRITER 1. A real sense of... I think, potential. I hate to say. A real sense of potential. I remember them vividly, you know. Those pages. I felt stirred by them. I won't lie. Even a little envious. That passage about the, who was it, the painter?

WRITER 2. Sculptor.

WRITER 1. Sculptor, yes. He... remind me?

WRITER 2. I don't...

WRITER 1. Something like... he gets fucked over by gallerists, he loses everything. Is homeless for a spell, and on the streets fashions these, how do you say, these abstract forms out of trash and carcasses.

WRITER 2....

WRITER 1. I remember. 'He built a roadside gallery of skeletal detritus.' The line sticks.

Beat.

Why'd you set it aside?

WRITER 2. It's been a very disabling year.

WRITER 1. Has it already been a year? Since the…

Beat.

WRITER 1 *starts up the video again.*

WRITER *2 gets up. Lights a cigarette.*

You were, I want to say, you were one of the… I suppose more passionate ones. Those salons. A real sort of –

WRITER 2 (*laughs*). Please.

WRITER 1. There was a real energy there. A real force. People were –

WRITER 2. It was a lot of bullshit. A lot of hot, angry bullshit. A lot of hot angry posturing bullshit.

WRITER 1. Bit harsh.

WRITER 2. Petitions and manifestos.

WRITER 1. It was *something.*

WRITER 2. Art protests.

WRITER 1. It was something.

WRITER 2. Most of them left.

WRITER 1. People have to… make difficult choices, you know how it was. Don't…

WRITER 2 *starts to laugh. Moments pass, then:*

WRITER 2. I actually thought a novel would… A fucking novel.

The video ends, there's rapturous applause.

WRITER 1. Can I have one?

WRITER 2 *hands* WRITER 1 *a cigarette.*

3. Street

PROTESTOR 1 *and* PROTESTOR 2, *gas masks hanging round their necks, are building a barricade. All the while,* PROTESTOR 1 *recounts:*

PROTESTOR 1. My favourite spot was under the old tree. In the backyard of the cafe. On Sundays. The old men would hang cages on the branches, cages with songbirds, and we'd all listen. Listen to the singing. Smoke, and drink. My grandfather did it, back in the day, keep songbirds, to keep him company when he worked. I've always loved them.

PROTESTOR 2. I hear them. (*Moving closer to hear.*) Ten clicks, it sounds. Hurry.

PROTESTOR 1. There was an old man who'd come by the cafe every Sunday. He had the most beautiful birds, glossy, and bright like flowers. He caught them himself. The singing was incredible, too. Like flutes. There I'd be, a cup of coffee, and the birds, under a tree. No one could tell me that wasn't paradise.

PROTESTOR 2. It's all bricks now. Funny when you think about it.

PROTESTOR 1. I asked him once, the old man, how he got the birds to sing like that. Said he started singing to them in the forests, when they were still wild. Crouching there, for hours, singing tunes. Eventually, they came to him. And then he took them.

They've formed a low wall of bricks.

PROTESTOR 2. Check it. You squat.

PROTESTOR 1 *squats behind the wall,* PROTESTOR 2 *lies prone.*

Too short. More. Hurry.

They rush to add some height to the wall. A loud sound goes off from the distance. It startles them.

Shit.

They finish a barricade, low and thick.

PROTESTOR 1. This will do.

PROTESTOR 2. Quick.

They hide behind it. Another loud sound goes off in the distance.

PROTESTOR 1. Last time I saw him, he already knew. He brought them here, his songbirds. One last time. Listened to them, tears in his eyes. Then opened the cages. None of them wanted to leave. So he starts singing. A funny old song. But it works. One by one, they fly.

PROTESTOR 2. Feels like so long ago. All of that.

PROTESTOR 2 *pulls on the gas mask.* PROTESTOR 1 *follows suit.*

Enter PROTESTOR 3, *running.*

PROTESTOR 3. Hurry.

They form up behind the barricade, and wait. Moments pass. PROTESTOR 1 *starts whistling a jaunty tune. Moments pass. The others join in nervously, and whistle as they look on. They hum.*

4. Party

At a dimly lit party. Loud music.

YOUNG WOMAN *enters from elsewhere in the party.* MAN *is sitting on a nearby couch, and watches* YOUNG WOMAN *for a few moments. Then:*

MAN. Nice party?

Beat.

Nice party?

YOUNG WOMAN. It's alright.

MAN. You flying?

YOUNG WOMAN. Flying?

MAN. High?

YOUNG WOMAN. Just booze and vibes.

MAN. I used to party like this myself in my day, but – a bit intense for a Christmas party, all this.

YOUNG WOMAN. Intense?

MAN. I'm too old, maybe.

YOUNG WOMAN. You here alone?

MAN. Possibly.

YOUNG WOMAN. Possibly?

MAN. Not sure where they are anymore. Came from another party. Bit intense, here, like I said.

YOUNG WOMAN. Did no one tell you this was an activist party?

MAN. Well, I had figured that out on my way in. What kind of activism?

YOUNG WOMAN. All sorts. I'm with student rent strike. But everyone's here. The network.

MAN. Marches?

YOUNG WOMAN. Sorry?

MAN. You organise marches.

YOUNG WOMAN. Sit-ins. Demos. Strikes. Bigger things than that, going forward.

MAN. You must be nineteen.

YOUNG WOMAN. Twenty.

MAN. Pretty.

YOUNG WOMAN. Sorry?

MAN. You're pretty.

YOUNG WOMAN. That's not appropriate.

MAN. I'm sorry. I apologise.

YOUNG WOMAN. It's okay.

Silence.

MAN. It was a compliment.

YOUNG WOMAN. Didn't ask for it.

MAN. Didn't have to.

Silence.

What's your name?

Silence.

You look like a nice girl. Some of the others here. Wild. Saw one girl near the toilet, so coked up, her face, covered in powder almost. I'm drunk. Sorry.

Silence.

I'm just being friendly.

YOUNG WOMAN. I think you need to fuck off.

MAN. Well.

YOUNG WOMAN. You and your starched shirt and cheap jacket, I mean. Can fuck off. And your words like pretty.

MAN. But you are.

YOUNG WOMAN. Fuck off.

MAN. I'll decide that for –

YOUNG WOMAN. Who brought you?

MAN. I came with a friend. Jodie.

YOUNG WOMAN. I don't know a Jodie. I'll say it again, this is a safe space, and you're not welcome here.

MAN. Safe space? A bunch of degenerates?

YOUNG WOMAN. Safe from people like you.

MAN. And what's people like me?

YOUNG WOMAN. You're embarrassing yourself.

   MAN *doesn't budge*.

MAN. Well in that case, I'm just going to stay right here.

   Silence. Then:

YOUNG WOMAN (*calling off*). Hey!

MAN. Who're you calling?

YOUNG WOMAN (*calling off*). Hello!

MAN. Calling for backup?

YOUNG WOMAN (*calling off*). Hey!

MAN. Listen. Don't do it.

YOUNG WOMAN. What?

MAN. Don't do it.

   Pause.

   Tomorrow.

   Silence.

   Yes. You don't have to.

   Silence.

YOUNG WOMAN. What?

MAN. You're amateurs. Kerosene in cans? In plain sight?

YOUNG WOMAN. How did you

MAN. You're young, barely twenty.

YOUNG WOMAN. How did you

MAN. Pretty girl like you, shouldn't get / mixed up in…

YOUNG WOMAN. Don't talk to me like –

MAN. Shouldn't get – hey, like I said, I used to be angry, at your age.

  YOUNG WOMAN *backs away.*

  You're scared.

YOUNG WOMAN. I...

MAN. You're not supposed to back away are you. What's the protocol?

YOUNG WOMAN. Protocol...

MAN. Smash, smash, smash?

YOUNG WOMAN. You're with...

MAN. I'm with all of them. Does it matter? Look love. Get your stuff. Get your best friend, run before things get

YOUNG WOMAN. Is something...

MAN. I know you're not that close to the –

YOUNG WOMAN. – I'm not with the...

MAN. The leader. The boy?

YOUNG WOMAN. The...

MAN. He's...

YOUNG WOMAN. He's not here.

MAN. Sure he is. (*Beat.*) People are coming. I'm letting you go.

  Silence.

YOUNG WOMAN. Letting – Why?

MAN. You're pretty.

  Pause.

  YOUNG WOMAN *advances a few paces.*

YOUNG WOMAN. What?

MAN. You're pretty.

YOUNG WOMAN *spits at* MAN.

YOUNG WOMAN. I'm not *pretty*. You

MAN. You are. Very much so. And I hate to see pretty girls caught up in things they don't

YOUNG WOMAN. Understand?

MAN. Have the balls to carry through.

YOUNG WOMAN. Fuck you.

MAN. Like one of those frightened piss-pants drug mules at airports. Shit out the coke in their arse before they even cross customs.

YOUNG WOMAN. You're bluffing. There's nothing

MAN. Got you worried.

YOUNG WOMAN (*calls off*). Someone!

MAN *stands*. YOUNG WOMAN *backs off*.

MAN. Go.

YOUNG WOMAN....

MAN. Now. Go.

YOUNG WOMAN *cannot move*.

MAN. This is the Left? Gathered in circles in the backyard jerking off to each other's outrage. Little undergrad kiddies fucking in strangers's bedrooms on the drugs they got with an allowance from daddy.

YOUNG WOMAN. You're bluffing. You're trolling.

MAN. You don't have to get mixed up in this. You don't.

YOUNG WOMAN *backs off*.

They're coming. Go.

YOUNG WOMAN *hesitates*.

No time to find anyone. Not even your boyfriend. I swear.

Beat.

YOUNG WOMAN (*dazed, making to leave*). When the time
   comes, we'll smash your head in first.

MAN. We'll see.

   Pause.

   YOUNG WOMAN *runs off, exits.* MAN *returns to the sofa.*

   MAN *finishes his drink.*

   He takes out his mobile.

5. Supermarket

MAN *chatters nervously at* CASHIER *as she charges his items.*

MAN. Got to eat, s'pose. (*Laughs.*)
   Reckon you lot might've done a sale,
   sort of...
   Given the... (*Gestures outside.*)
   Joking.
   But you got to eat, hey?
   Myself, I'm making a sort of
   stew I think.
   Given the circumstances (*Laughs.*)
   Got to eat.
   Nothing fatalistic 'bout anything, is there?
   Practical, more like,
   'bout having to eat.
   Got to eat, that's my dad
   my dad always, y'know
   he said... he was the sort to
   yell at us, if we even dared to
   walk as we ate
   even a sandwich, he'd always...
   short of shoving a fork and knife at us
   he'd say

'sit down and eat your
fucking sandwich.
'S an insult to the cook
and to the food not least
to yourself,
walking and eating,
is life that desperate?
Even a cow stops to graze,
So sit down
and eat your fucking sandwich.'
Dad, he was a proper
sense of occasion
kind of man.
He said his dad was like that too,
obviously,
said his dad was, I mean they were
dirt poor, yeah,
growing up...
And dad tells this story
about the five of them
in the old days,
sitting at a table to share
a slice of...
something or another
piece of meat or
something miserable...
cabbage or
a single potato
slicing it up into portions
fork and knife
making all the
noises...
'mm
delicious
thank you
pass the salt.'

Beat.

Always got to eat.

Last thing he did was eat.
Naturally, y'know?
Just last year.

CASHIER. Sorry.

MAN. It was grand.
Hospital cracker.
Butter.
Which is to say
You've got to eat,
And make a thing of it, y'know?
Dad would say, and
you wouldn't think
a bland little biscuit and
some butter…
Margarine…

CASHIER. Sorry.

MAN. It's alright.
In a way I'm glad he's gone
You know?
There's some hungers
That just aren't right.
You know?
Some hungers're totally
senseless
sandy biscuits
smelly shelters
stomachs like dust…
Dad would say
you *still* gotta eat but
he would'a hated all this.

Pause.
'nway.
Stew, y'know?
Woke up today, thinking
Heard the news, thinking
Thinking I've got no appetite
But I want to make a stew.

I sort of understand now,
my dad, that is,
his point of view,
I do, really, it's…

CASHIER. Can't take that away.

MAN. Yeah. Yeah.

CASHIER. They can but…

MAN. They can but they can't, yeah.

Beat.

CASHIER. Looks like a nice stew.

MAN. Yeah?

CASHIER. Simple.

A siren, outside. They pause to listen to it.

I didn't charge the sausages.

MAN. Oh.

CASHIER. It's eighty eight fifty.

MAN. Thanks.

MAN *pays and takes the bags.*

CASHIER. You'll be fine.

MAN. Thanks.

CASHIER. You'll be fine.

6. Garden

At night. A garden. WIFE *is busy planting bulbs in a patch of soil.* HUSBAND *stands aside, watching, holding a large suitcase.*

HUSBAND. Darling.

WIFE. Don't hurry me.

HUSBAND. I'm sorry.

WIFE. I've started them too late.

HUSBAND. No you haven't. It's warmer this year.

WIFE. They won't last. They'll rot before they sprout.

HUSBAND. They'll be fine.

WIFE. I knew I should have done them last month.

HUSBAND. They'll be beautiful when we come back.

WIFE. You don't know that.

Beat.

HUSBAND. Can I help?

WIFE. Don't rush me.

HUSBAND. Please.

WIFE. Just a few more.

Silence as WIFE *finishes planting.*

Is that all you're packing?

HUSBAND. Yes.

WIFE. Is that for just you, or for…

HUSBAND. Both of us. We ought to pack light.

Pause.

WIFE. They bloom at different times. Some of them sooner.
There'll be some blooms. Eventually.

HUSBAND. That's something.

WIFE. Can't we bring another bag?

HUSBAND. No.

Silence.

WIFE. I've got to wash my hands now.

WIFE *makes to exit.*

HUSBAND. Please hurry.

WIFE *stops and turns back. She looks at the flower patch.*

WIFE. Growing up he was a good boy.

HUSBAND. I know.

WIFE. A clever boy. Always doing the right thing sort of boy, always saying the right thing.

HUSBAND. I know.

WIFE. He would ride with me in the car, you know, as I did the shopping. Chatter away next to me like he was giving a commentary on the street.

HUSBAND. I know.

WIFE. Never thought chattering would do him in.

Silence.

HUSBAND. He called me. Last week. You know.

WIFE. You said.

HUSBAND. Told him I couldn't listen anymore. Every time. It froze my heart over, the things he said.

WIFE. You should have…

HUSBAND.…

WIFE. You could have…

Silence.

If I'd planted them last month there might've been flowers today.

HUSBAND. We can't have…

WIFE. He would plant these with me, you know. When he was little.

HUSBAND. I know.

WIFE. His chubby fingers, he'd claw into the soil. He used to love when they shot up. All the colours. He'd draw them with crayons on paper.

HUSBAND. I remember.

WIFE. Every time. This garden. A little boy in the garden.

HUSBAND. I remember. (*Beat.*) Your hands.

WIFE. Oh, right.

WIFE *makes to leave again. She stops and turns.*

HUSBAND. That's all we can do now.

WIFE. I saw it, you know. All this.

HUSBAND. When?

WIFE. The last time he came.

HUSBAND. You saw…

WIFE. Sat across from me at the table nursing his coffee. In that way he does. Looking at it. Not really drinking it.

HUSBAND. I know that look.

WIFE. He looked older. His shoulders sagged. I should've known. He knew. He was afraid.

HUSBAND. I heard it in his voice.

WIFE. You heard?

HUSBAND. I did. Over the phone.

Silence.

WIFE. We should have tied up him, kept him here, stopped him going back. Should have fed him to death. Better to have eaten to death than…

HUSBAND. Come on.

WIFE. It's too late. I'm sorry. I'm sorry.

HUSBAND. You cannot…

A car rumbles up in the distance.

Pause.

That's…

WIFE. Let me – I'm a mess. Oh. No, I ought to water them first.

The car horn sounds. HUSBAND *and* WIFE *start.*

HUSBAND. Come.

WIFE. You go. I'll catch up. Hurry.

    HUSBAND *embraces* WIFE. HUSBAND *takes the bag and exits.*

    WIFE *starts to water the bulbs.*

    Grow. Please. I know it's too late. I love you. I miss you. I'm sorry. I love you. I miss you. I'm sorry.

    HUSBAND *returns. Watches this ritual.*

    HUSBAND *hugs* WIFE.

    Silence except for the sound of a boot opening, being loaded, and closing. Then:

HUSBAND. We ought to pray.

WIFE. Yes.

    They pray silently.

    The car horn sounds.

HUSBAND. We have to go.

WIFE. I can't.

HUSBAND. We must, before…

WIFE. I can't.

    The car horn sounds.

HUSBAND. They're waiting.

WIFE. I can't.

7. Wall

MALE SOLDIER *and* FEMALE SOLDIER *are standing by a wall*.

MALE SOLDIER. This one's got nuts in it.

FEMALE SOLDIER. Thanks. You didn't have to.

MALE SOLDIER. I wanted to.

FEMALE SOLDIER. You wanted

MALE SOLDIER. A chocolate break.

FEMALE SOLDIER. Oh. Cheers.

MALE SOLDIER. Cheers.

They eat the squishy chocolate bars in silence for a few moments.

Did you ever drink something called Milo?

FEMALE SOLDIER. Milo?

MALE SOLDIER. Like a chocolate drink.

FEMALE SOLDIER. Like Nesquik?

MALE SOLDIER. A bit. This tastes like Milo. Add that to the list. Of things I miss.

First thing I'll do when it's over is get some Milo.

FEMALE SOLDIER. You really like chocolate, don't you?

MALE SOLDIER. You have anyone?

FEMALE SOLDIER. Anyone

MALE SOLDIER. Back home.

FEMALE SOLDIER. I don't know.

MALE SOLDIER. How do you not know?

FEMALE SOLDIER. Anymore.

MALE SOLDIER. Oh. Chocolate's melty.

FEMALE SOLDIER. It's the heat. From your body.

> MALE SOLDIER *gets intimately close to* FEMALE SOLDIER.

MALE SOLDIER. You like that?

FEMALE SOLDIER. What?

MALE SOLDIER. Not too warm?

FEMALE SOLDIER. Think we might play some music?

MALE SOLDIER. They'll hear.

FEMALE SOLDIER. We're the only ones.

> *A jaunty pop track plays.*

> He's got a beautiful voice.

> *They eat chocolate and listen to music.*

> Should spend more time listening to music 'stead of shooting at people.

MALE SOLDIER. I quite like it.

FEMALE SOLDIER. What?

MALE SOLDIER. This war. Bit like an adventure. Never would've seen trees like this back home. This heat. These smells. These noises. That face.

FEMALE SOLDIER. You're flirting.

MALE SOLDIER. Plus it's fun shooting at those assholes. Saw a platoon of them blown up with a bomb like bits of red popcorn once. Got to admire that.

> *Beat.*

> Look, chocolate's nice, but are we going to do it or not?

FEMALE SOLDIER. Do...

> MALE SOLDIER *licks* FEMALE SOLDIER's *arm.*

MALE SOLDIER. Can I kiss you?

They kiss. As they kiss, the lights slowly come up behind the wall.

REFUGEE *is crouching behind it, terrified.*

REFUGEE *has been listening this whole time.*

REFUGEE *detecting that the* SOLDIERS *are distracted, readies for flight. Then:*

FEMALE SOLDIER. I can't.

MALE SOLDIER. Why not.

FEMALE SOLDIER. I've got someone.

MALE SOLDIER. You said you didn't know that.

FEMALE SOLDIER. I've got someone.

MALE SOLDIER. Feeling guilty?

FEMALE SOLDIER.We made promises. No point fighting if we can't hang on to things like that.

MALE SOLDIER. Seriously.

FEMALE SOLDIER. Sorry.

MALE SOLDIER. You came out here for more than chocolate.

FEMALE SOLDIER. I know.

MALE SOLDIER. I'm sad.

FEMALE SOLDIER. Why?

MALE SOLDIER. I thought. Well. We've been making eyes, haven't we? For weeks.

FEMALE SOLDIER. I suppose.

MALE SOLDIER. You don't make eyes and then...

FEMALE SOLDIER. Come on let's go back.

MALE SOLDIER. Look, I'm gonna kiss you.

FEMALE SOLDIER. No.

MALE SOLDIER. You owe it. For flirting.

FEMALE SOLDIER. What?

MALE SOLDIER. Oh come on, what happens out here doesn't count.

FEMALE SOLDIER. Seriously, fuck off.

> MALE SOLDIER *pins* FEMALE SOLDIER *down.*
> *They struggle. It gets very violent. Eventually,* FEMALE
> SOLDIER *manages to overpower* MALE SOLDIER, *and in
> the chaos,* REFUGEE *takes the opportunity to make a run for
> it. Startled,* FEMALE SOLDIER *jumps off* MALE SOLDIER
> *and shoots* REFUGEE *dead.* MALE SOLDIER *gets up and
> rounds on* FEMALE SOLDIER.

MALE SOLDIER. What the fuck was that?

> *In a panic,* FEMALE SOLDIER *shoots* MALE SOLDIER
> *dead. Two dead bodies.*

8. Refuge

REFUGEE 1 *and* REFUGEE 2 *are sitting around the glow of an
electric lamp, drinking hot drinks. In the distance, the sporadic
sounds of passing aircraft.*

REFUGEE 1. I remember a time when the art museum would
let us in for free on Fridays. There'd be a queue that snaked
around for the whole afternoon.

My mother, she was a devotee. She was determined to raise
me properly. I think many immigrant mothers were like that.
Especially the ones whose kids never lived through the boats.
The searchlights.

My mum tried to cover my eyes with art. She would bring
me there every Friday. Sit. Lost, staring at some painting or
another. I hated that place.

There was this one piece of art. This hideous black mass of twisted nails, concertina wire, a block of asphalt brushed over with some kind of paint. Resin. Always, on the way out, always, before we left, she would call at this monstrosity.

'It's very important. Such an important artist'. Mind you, this was twisted nails, concertina wire, and a block of asphalt. 'Very important,' and we'd stand there, as if in prayer, for a good long time, and then leave.

A noise from outside. They start.

REFUGEE 2. Turn that off.

REFUGEE 1 *turns off the light. They move to crouch in the dark, waiting as something passes.*

REFUGEE 1. The art museum was the first thing they took. Set it off on Friday when it was full of people. Mum had long died, or we'd have been blown up too, I reckon.

I watched the news. All that angry, smoking rubble. A great mountain of nails, wire, asphalt. A mountain of burnt art. And I remember thinking, in the heat of all that violence: yes, mum, this is important. These shapes. Truly, finally, important.

REFUGEE 2. Quiet.

REFUGEE 1. Later I found out he was a minor artist from the old country. The asphalt artist. The piece was called 'Farewell'. In mum's language. Apparently, he had picked up the whole damned thing, fully formed, before he fled. Imagine that. Fleeing for your life. And you bring along a block of asphalt?

REFUGEE 2. Shh.

REFUGEE 1. Artists, hey?

REFUGEE 2 . Shh.

9. Street

A murmuration of birds. Crows and ravens. The ruins of a city.
CITIZEN 1, *elderly, lies badly injured amongst the rubble.*
CITIZEN 2, *much younger and closer to death, lies whimpering*
next to CITIZEN 1. SOLDIER *feeds* CITIZEN 1 *water from a*
tankard.

SOLDIER. It's safe now.

CITIZEN 1. There were TV news people.

SOLDIER. It's over.

CITIZEN 1. Was I on TV?

SOLDIER. It's over now.

CITIZEN 1. Are my limbs intact?

SOLDIER. You're badly cut.

    CITIZEN 2 *moans.*

CITIZEN 1. Give him water

SOLDIER. He won't make it….

CITIZEN 1. He'll dry out if / you don't.

SOLDIER. From the looks of…
    Shit.

CITIZEN 1 (*straining to hear*). 'r those birds?

SOLDIER (*to* CITIZEN 1). Listen, you need to conserve your
    energy.

CITIZEN 1. Birds. Crows.

SOLDIER. Crows.

CITIZEN 1. They've come back.

SOLDIER. Shh.

CITIZEN 1. Used to be an old tree here.

SOLDIER. It'll be a while,
    before we can get you two...

CITIZEN 1. They've come back.
    Clever bastards.

    CITIZEN 2 *moans*.

SOLDIER. He's not gonna...
    I don't...
    He's split open.
    'S a miracle he's...

CITIZEN 1. Listen, they're singing...

    CITIZEN 2 *moans*.

SOLDIER. Fuck.
    Should he... do we
    I dunno. Shit, he's split open.

CITIZEN 1. Coming home songs...
    Singing...
    The war's over for them too.

    Beat.

    The president, what...
    Hey?

SOLDIER. What?

CITIZEN 1. The –

SOLDIER. Gunned down.
    In his office.
    Not long. Just...
    (*To* CITIZEN 2.) Can you...
    Shit.

CITIZEN 1. They should parade the fucker.

SOLDIER. What?

CITIZEN 1. Parade him through the streets.

    CITIZEN 2 *moans, harder now.*

SOLDIER. Oh god.

CITIZEN 1. Let them shit on him.
  The birds.

SOLDIER. He's in so much pain.

CITIZEN 1. Big swooping shits.

  SOLDIER *goes up to* CITIZEN 2.

  Something transpires between them.

SOLDIER (*to* CITIZEN 2). I'm sorry.
  I'm sorry.

CITIZEN 1. His face. Caked with shit.

SOLDIER (*to* CITIZEN 2). You…

CITIZEN 1. Fucking erase his face with shit.

  SOLDIER *nods at* CITIZEN 2.

CITIZEN 1. 'S the least he deserves.

  SOLDIER *readies his rifle.*

  The least…

  SOLDIER *shoots* CITIZEN 2 *dead.*

  Silence. Then the bird-calls resume.

SOLDIER. I'm sorry.

CITIZEN 1. They smell blood.

SOLDIER. He was…

CITIZEN 1. Here they come.

SOLDIER. Shit.

CITIZEN 1. A murder of crows.

SOLDIER. No, no…

  SOLDIER *shoots into the air, trying to scare the crows away.*
  A cascade of feathers.

CITIZEN 1. Let them.

SOLDIER. Get away.

CITIZEN 1. They've suffered.
And they had no words to suffer with,
imagine that.

The birds descend. SOLDIER *continues to shoot at them, but they are relentless.*

PART TWO

1. Memorial

*Thirty years later. In the shadow of a massive war memorial,
a marvel of shining glass.* GUIDE *stands aside addressing an
unseen group of visitors.*

GUIDE. No photographs. Please. Out of respect. Old beliefs
about photography are honoured here.

When designed, it was considered, this structure, a spiritual
totem as well as an architectural feature. Glass was chosen as
the principal material. For the incandescence of sunrise. And
at night to resemble a pitch black obsidian obelisk.

Light pollution from surrounding buildings was a problem in
the first few years, but regulation is now in place. The poetics
of it, this glass shard daily shining out from the darkness, I
think, are clear.

The reflective surface, up close, is, coated with an iridescent
resin. The effect is, as you can imagine...

Some people have reported sightings. Of the lost, and fallen.
Others see their own faces. Broken, and distorted.

Others see a fresco of twisted bodies.

This after all was the site of the... well. We needn't revisit
that.

You all will have seen the photographic accounts of the
damage. Some of the older generation call this a haunted
place. You don't need a belief in the supernatural to
understand.

On a quiet day, some say if you listen carefully, you can hear
sounds. Whether from the structure itself or something else,
it's unclear. Fluttering, beating wings.

A low groaning.

What they hear, chanting, lamenting, crying for help, praying, it's not clear.

It's all nonsense of course. At least I think so. You can listen if you want.

See if you hear anything.

2. Studio

A fashion house. COUTURIERE, *is in a meeting with her* ASSISTANT, *as well as* CONSULTANT 1 *and* CONSULTANT 2.

CONSULTANT 1. Flowers are in again.

COUTURIERE. Flowers?

CONSULTANT 1. Or they will be. Natural motifs and bright colours rank high on our surveys.

CONSULTANT 2. Across all age groups.

ASSISTANT. Flowers. Which? Crocuses? Lilies? Roses?

CONSULTANT 1. Whichever. Moods are on the upswing.

CONSULTANT 2. Postwar renaissance.

COUTURIERE. Flowers.

CONSULTANT 2. They're symptomatic of a larger trend, you must understand. It's not just flowers. Bigger, bolder, brighter. Extravagant. Opulent. Gilded. Baroque.

ASSISTANT. I like that. We can work with that.

CONSULTANT 1. Homeless chic is the emperor's new clothes. Austerity is a bore. Minimalism is a waste of money. If people are buying fashion, they're buying big ideas.

Transformation. Radical self-expression. Rebirth. Look at our cross-market analysis. Here. Home-ownership is up. Gardens are back in. People are gardening again. Getting in touch with the seasons.

COUTURIERE. Flowers. Shit. Never a dull day in the office.

ASSISTANT. We could do some low-cost tulle and organza features.

CONSULTANT 2. Also raspberry.

COUTURIERE. Raspberry?

CONSULTANT 1. Colour trends. Raspberry.

ASSISTANT. So, pink flowers?

COUTURIERE. Jesus.

CONSULTANT 2. The palette of the past ten or so years has not afforded much in the reds. We've seen long passages of black and grey. But the time for mourning is... well incomes and moods are on the upswing.

ASSISTANT. Raspberry is very versatile.

COUTURIERE. So... paisley and chintz.

Pause.

CONSULTANT 1. Not necessarily.

COUTURIERE. You've come in to tell me, basically, paisley and chintz.

Pause.

CONSULTANT 1. We're looking at celebratory indices. Sparkle, pomp. Sequins and shimmer trim. To match trends in pop music. Party pop. Flowers and party pop. Raspberry. We're telling our clients in the restaurant biz as well. Cocktails, desserts. Jewelled pastries. Frosted flowers. Tart, spring flavours.

COUTURIERE *groans.*

ASSISTANT. Trend prediction isn't about literal specifics, you know that.

COUTURIERE. You calling me stupid now?

ASSISTANT. No.

CONSULTANT 2. Space travel is also picking up on our –

COUTURIERE. Space travel.

CONSULTANT 1. Space travel. Futurism. Robots. Inter-
dimensionality. Science fiction moods.

ASSISTANT. We've purchased some holographic gauze, we
could –

COUTURIERE. I look at my collections, and I see years of
urban soldiers, captains of revolution, ravers, and iconoclasts.
Generations. You mean to tell me this is somehow irrelevant.

CONSULTANT 2. Trend-wise, yes.

COUTURIERE. I do not think it's irrelevant.

Pause.

CONSULTANT 1. Well since this is a high fashion label, we
were looking at luxury indices.

COUTURIERE. You're calling me cheap, now?

CONSULTANT 1. Not at all.

COUTURIERE. I am not in the business of helping people fit
in.

ASSISTANT. That's not what they're –

COUTURIERE. People seem to think it's in good taste to wear
colour again. Fine. Whatever. But then they mock me. Black
again? I know it. They call my clothes burial shrouds. I
know they think I'm a relic. Maybe I am. Or maybe I just
remember more deeply.

Pause.

Well they can fuck off. And you can fuck off. With your
upswings.

CONSULTANT 2. These are the trends, we're just reporting.

COUTURIERE. I'm bored.

CONSULTANT 1. People just want to have a good time.

COUTURIERE. You can have a good time in black.

CONSULTANT 2. We're not disputing that, we're...

COUTURIERE. Take your paisley and chintz and space-ships, and go. This is over.

CONSULTANT 1 *and* CONSULTANT 2 *exit. After a moment:*

ASSISTANT. Don't be so stubborn. We could try and work some florals in. Subtly.

COUTURIERE. I hate flowers.

Silence.

You should have known better.

ASSISTANT. I'm trying to be positive.

Silence.

COUTURIERE. My mother was a wonderful gardener, you know. She grew flowers in the garden.

ASSISTANT. Lovely.

COUTURIERE. They shot my mother in her garden. They took my father, but shot her in the face. The neighbours told us later they had to bury her in the flower patch to stop the stench.

When the war ended, and we managed to find our way home, you know what we saw? A garden in full bloom. Absurdly colourful flowers spilling over the fence.

ASSISTANT. I'm sorry.

COUTURIERE. They'll grow through anything. Flowers. I hate them. No flowers.

ASSISTANT....

COUTURIERE. No flowers.

3. Gallery

An art gallery.

Two artists, embrace. MENTOR *is older than* ARTIST.

ARTIST.You've gotten fat.

They laugh.

MENTOR. I wouldn't have recognised you if it weren't for the banners outside.

ARTIST. Have you seen everything?

MENTOR. Yes I was given the tour.

ARTIST. What do you think?

Pause.

MENTOR. It's so white here.

ARTIST. Yes.

MENTOR. So bright. It's all yours?

ARTIST. Yes. All mine.

MENTOR. These years of work. You've done well for yourself.

Pause.

ARTIST. Where are you staying?

MENTOR. In a hotel.

ARTIST. Have you eaten?

MENTOR. I don't like the food here. Do you?

ARTIST. It's an acquired taste.

MENTOR. Which is your favourite?

ARTIST. What?

MENTOR. Of these pieces?

ARTIST. They all work together. Hard to say. What do you think?

MENTOR. They like our stories.

Beat.

ARTIST. Who?

MENTOR. The people here. They like our stories.

ARTIST. Yes.

MENTOR. Helps them feel connected to it all. The war. History.

ARTIST. Yes.

MENTOR. Something urgent. Concrete.

ARTIST....

MENTOR. You should have stuck to painting.

Silence.

You have a gift for sentiment. These abstract shapes...

ARTIST. They are sentimental...

MENTOR. No one laments anymore. It's uncouth to lament. It's easier to twist things into odd shapes.

ARTIST. Not easier...

MENTOR. Not easier. Fashionable.

Silence.

When will you come home?

ARTIST. I've made this my home.

MENTOR. The food is so watery, though.

Silence.

They would welcome you back.

ARTIST. I know.

MENTOR. Throw a ceremony. You would be garlanded.
Another of these retrospectives. They say your pieces sell.

ARTIST. They do.

MENTOR. Very well.

ARTIST. I –

MENTOR. Do they sit, in the houses of rich men, who've never suffered like we have?

Beat.

ARTIST. I won't apologise for it.

MENTOR. No, of course you mustn't.

ARTIST. You've come to mock me?

Pause.

MENTOR. No. I'm sorry. It's just hard for me, seeing this. Our home, refracted like this. Plastic. False.

ARTIST. It's true to me.

MENTOR. Seen from far away.

ARTIST. I've watched things intently. From afar, but with no less –

MENTOR. You were wise to leave. And stay away.

ARTIST. I know.

MENTOR. But maybe it's time to come back.

Silence.

They have no need for you here.

ARTIST. That's...

MENTOR. Here you're just another war-ravaged show-pony.

ARTIST. It's not that simple.

MENTOR. And you profit from it. They do. But not us. Thirty years and you've not once set foot in our country.

ARTIST. I lost so much trying to leave. It's impossible to retrace. Those steps. There's so much grief.

Silence.

MENTOR. Is this the shape of your grief?

ARTIST. What?

MENTOR (*gesturing around*). Is this the shape of your grief?

ARTIST. Yes.

MENTOR. Do people weep when they see them?

ARTIST. Weep?

MENTOR. They stand and contemplate?

ARTIST. Yes.

MENTOR. They take photographs.

ARTIST. Yes.

MENTOR. They come in droves.

   Silence.

   Those were terrible days.

ARTIST. It's all here.

MENTOR. Then where are the rotting corpses?

ARTIST. That's a cliché.

MENTOR. The hollowed faces?

ARTIST. I am not a documentarian.

MENTOR. The shit and vomit?

   Silence.

   Have you asked yourself? / Is it adequate to the task?

ARTIST. Please, we haven't seen each other...

MENTOR. Are you? Adequate to the task. I have not dared to give shape to my grief. Few of us have. No one would be able to look at it. Let alone take a photo of it.

   Silence.

ARTIST. There was a woman I fled with. She died as we passed the eastern border. A bit of her skull flew into the air as she did.

MENTOR. Is it here? Did you make art out of a woman's skull?

ARTIST. No. It's my most private belonging. It's the shape of my
grief.

Silence.

MENTOR. And all of this?

4. Tele

A FATHER *and his* CHILD *watching something play on the
news, on the sofa.*

FATHER. They're all...
 They're always...
 You can see that can't you?
 Always doing this to themselves
 Always... see it's in their
 History, isn't it...
 I mean look at it...
 Their lot...
 Always in trouble.
 It's always been in their...
 Yeah, there's something in there,
 somehow
 always making them...
 causing all of this.
 Now I'm not saying it's not awful
 Not saying it's fair,
 And not saying they're *all*...
 Each and every one?
 Not saying that at all.
 You hear?
 Individually, I've known them
 Some of them
 to be quite nice
 the modern ones,

the thinking
educated ones, obviously
richer than us, it's sometimes
possible, you'll sometimes see that,
more posh than us sometimes
you see them on tele, sometimes,
you know, holding their own
professorial-like, nice folks,
sometimes.
It's because they know
these nice ones,
know, see, how you're meant to...
how the world works,
know how to make up for

CHILD. The nast–

FATHER. not nastiness,
     the handicap.
     it's knowing your handicap
     isn't it?
     'S what I'm always telling you,
     work with your...
     Can't say life threw us the best hand
     Can you?

CHILD. No.

FATHER. But we make it work.
     Don't we?
     There are people who
     will tell you otherwise,
     about these things
     'course there are,
     But you've got to make up
     your own mind sometimes,
     and I'm telling you:
     What's good for them
     is not good for us.
     It's a bad mix,
     it's a bad idea,

bad *politics*
if you ask me.
Watch enough
you'll see.
See how it's always
the ones you don't trust
the cocky ones
with sneers
it's always them
saying
open arms and what not.
Open arms.
Never once in the history of...
If you think about it
Since ancient times...
never once was that a good idea,
to open your arms,
was it,
that's just common sense
isn't it?
You wouldn't, would you?
At least I hope not.

CHILD. When you say sneer...

FATHER. 'S when you smell something
You don't like.

CHILD. Yeah.

FATHER. Don't let people sneer at you.
I don't like that one bit
Makes you feel stupid
And small doesn't it?
When it's you who has
the common sense to..
For wanting...
Such as nice times, like
Like the one we're having now.
Wanting not to be dead
Knife in your head...

He holds CHILD *close.*

Wouldn't want that
Not to you
Or Mum.
Anyone.
Do you think I'm a good father?

CHILD. Mm hmm.

Companionable silence.

He's bleeding.

FATHER. He is.

Enter MOTHER.

MOTHER. Time for bed

FATHER. Aw, but we're…

MOTHER. It's late

FATHER. We're bonding aren't we?

MOTHER (*to* CHILD). Your dad talking your ear off?

(*To* FATHER.) Would you 'least put something else on?

Miserable stuff, the news.

FATHER. Not just the news.
It's life, isn't that right?
An education.
Isn't that right?

5. School

An office. Outside, the sound of schoolchildren. A young
TEACHER *sits across from the* PRINCIPAL. *The* PRINCIPAL
pushes some documents towards the TEACHER.

PRINCIPAL. You should've consulted me first.

TEACHER. You said I'd have full autonomy –

PRINCIPAL. Within reasonable boundaries.

TEACHER. What's so unreasonable about this?

PRINCIPAL. These poems. Here. And this one.

Pause.

What I think, personally, doesn't matter.

TEACHER. What's the issue?

PRINCIPAL. But this is not coming from me. It's upstairs.

TEACHER. I don't understand.

PRINCIPAL. To include him in a course about national
    literature –

TEACHER. This is national literature. / How not to include…

PRINCIPAL. Yes! Yes. I've read him. We all have.

TEACHER. Then you can see why he's on the list.

PRINCIPAL. It's tricky, is all I'm saying.

TEACHER. And these poems?

PRINCIPAL. He's got other poems.

TEACHER. None like these.

PRINCIPAL. These being the controversial ones.

TEACHER. Controversial. To be clear, we're talking about
    poetry?

PRINCIPAL. You've always had a knack for… Listen. Do you
    ever stop to think that these ideas might be… Stop to think
    how… these are children we're dealing with. Young minds.
    Yes?

TEACHER. Yes.

PRINCIPAL. They take peace for granted. We all do, on some
    level, but the children most of all.

TEACHER. We're still talking about poetry, yes?

PRINCIPAL. Yes.

TEACHER. A few poems aren't going to –

PRINCIPAL. A few *ideas*. Remind yourself. Our history.

TEACHER. What ideas? In the poem. Show me. Please.

PRINCIPAL. This one. It declares that the country is like a fat farm animal drunk on grain alcohol.

TEACHER. He means forgetful. Amnesiac.

PRINCIPAL. A farm animal. Piggish. Stupid. Reared for its meat. Brains enriched with honey water. Questionable even as poetry. And the sentiment. It's not nice. Unpatriotic.

TEACHER. Unpatriotic? That's not at all –

PRINCIPAL. And this one. Pontiffs with countenances of perpetual sorrow. It's so transparent. How is it right to talk about our leaders this way? And what do we mean, teaching children caricature?

TEACHER. We are no longer that country.

PRINCIPAL. No, but peace is fragile. That is the sentiment upstairs.

Beat.

You're not naive.

TEACHER. I'm sorry?

PRINCIPAL. You know you can't simply push these things through like that.

TEACHER. I don't know that.

PRINCIPAL. Yes. You do. And still. And so I think, maybe, you've got something to say. Do you? You're free to, obviously. But in your personal capacity. Even then.

Silence.

The sentiment upstairs is that he's a watched figure. A subversive.

TEACHER. A *subversive*? In this day and age?

PRINCIPAL. Not *subversive*. Per se. One to watch. To be a little wary of. Whose views are questionable. Problematic. His intent is dubious. Slanted. Uncharitable. Unpatriotic.

TEACHER. He's free to be all those things if he wants.

PRINCIPAL. He is, of course. But you, we…

Silence.

TEACHER. This is very disturbing.

PRINCIPAL. Talk to me.

TEACHER. I… don't know what to say. It's very regressive.

PRINCIPAL. It's easier to just remove him.

TEACHER. There's no reason to.

PRINCIPAL. I've laid it out.

TEACHER. You haven't.

PRINCIPAL. You're putting me in a difficult position.

TEACHER. If anything happens, and why *should* anything happen, then I will answer for it.

PRINCIPAL (*laughs*). You're paranoid. Answer? There is no one to answer to.

Beat.

TEACHER. What?

PRINCIPAL. We don't live in those times anymore.

TEACHER. What?

PRINCIPAL. I'm just advising you.

TEACHER. Upstairs, you said.

PRINCIPAL. I'm strongly advising you.

TEACHER. It's just poetry.

PRINCIPAL. These are sensitive times. We've got to be
    judicious about our criticism. Does it do anyone any good?
    Is it constructive? Does it shake faith in our leaders? They're
    not perfect. Who is? Don't make things difficult for yourself.

   Silence.

TEACHER. I won't do it. It has to come from you. Or them.
    Whatever. It can't be from me. Not without –

PRINCIPAL. Your principles.

TEACHER. Yes.

PRINCIPAL. I understand.

TEACHER. We understand each other. You make the cuts. Not
    me.

   Silence.

PRINCIPAL. You were always going to be a risky hire. I knew
    that. From the start. Your docket.

TEACHER. My docket?

PRINCIPAL. The kinds of clearances we had to do, you have no
    idea. But here we are. I knew we'd have this talk eventually.
    It's been two years, hasn't it? The students love you. We all
    love you. Nice to have actual artists in the mix. Adds colour.
    But you've got to know, now I suppose as good a time as
    any, that there are things we cannot do. Lines not to cross.
    You're friends with him?

TEACHER. What?

PRINCIPAL. You and him. You're friends. Yes.

TEACHER. We got to know each other / writing plays.

PRINCIPAL. The theatre. Yes. His *plays*. More than in his
    poems, he really goes for it. I've seen them. I've seen yours.

TEACHER. You have?

PRINCIPAL. Not that much to worry about, if I'm being honest.
    Lightweight. A little banal. Hiding behind metaphors. But
    still. Naughty stuff. Very critical.

TEACHER. I don't see…

PRINCIPAL. I have to tell you, very simply, you get what you ask for. Writing the things you do.

TEACHER. They're just plays.

PRINCIPAL *takes back the document and makes three very hard strikes on it.*

PRINCIPAL. Lucky for you I've not sent this upstairs.

TEACHER. I –

PRINCIPAL (*making notes on the document*). It's done, yes? We're agreed. (*Beat.*) Tell me. You've fucked.

TEACHER. What?

PRINCIPAL. The two of you.

TEACHER. I –

PRINCIPAL (*handing* TEACHER *the document*). Thank you.

Silence.

6. Prison

WARDEN *has just passed* PATIENT, *older, some pills.*

WARDEN. It's part of the procedure.

PATIENT. The procedure. Is that what they're calling it.

WARDEN. Well you can call it what you want.

PATIENT *doesn't take the pill.*

PATIENT. Why have you been so kind to me?

WARDEN. It's my job.

PATIENT. Thank you.

WARDEN. The lethal dose will be two hours after you take this pill.

PATIENT. What's this, then?

WARDEN. It's ecstasy.

PATIENT....

WARDEN. First this pill, then the other.

PATIENT. I took one of these. Back in the day.

WARDEN. Do you understand?

PATIENT. At a party. In someone's house. In a city I don't remember. On holiday.

WARDEN. Makes it more...

Pause.

PATIENT. My lover was there. Egging me on.

WARDEN. If you take it now, it'll time just right.

PATIENT....

WARDEN. It's not my...

PATIENT. I'm not

WARDEN....

PATIENT. It was war. I'm not a bad person.

WARDEN. It'll be alright.

PATIENT. I don't want to take it. Not like this. Not before the...

WARDEN....

PATIENT. It reminds me too much of...

WARDEN. Of what?

PATIENT. Of dancing. Of parties. Of kissing.

Pause.

WARDEN. How old were you?

PATIENT. Twenty-eight.

WARDEN. In a city.

PATIENT. In the winter. New Year's Eve.

WARDEN. With

PATIENT. My lover.

WARDEN. And?

PATIENT. There were fireworks. They set them off from the streets and the rooftops. It was beautiful. Fire in the sky. Sign of the times, but we didn't know it then. I closed my eyes, there were fireworks in my head. And loud music. We danced. It was like learning to breathe for the very first time.

PATIENT *closes his eyes and hums a song.*

WARDEN *slips the pill into his mouth.*

7. Truck

The back of a cargo truck. In motion. A PARENT *and* CHILD, *huddling in the dark. They are already dead. The container is suffused with these last moments.*

CHILD. It's cold.

PARENT. I know.

CHILD. It's so cold.

PARENT. Come.

CHILD. I'm so hungry.

PARENT. I know.

CHILD. Why can't we eat?

PARENT. Soon.

CHILD. Why didn't we eat?

PARENT. There was no time.

CHILD. Lying.

PARENT. There wasn't.

CHILD. It's so we don't shit.

Silence.

PARENT. Don't talk about that. It's not nice.

CHILD. How long more.

PARENT. Not much longer.

CHILD. Lying. You don't know.

PARENT. It's been so long, we must be closer. Every time it
    stops, we are closer. How many times now, have we stopped?

CHILD. Five.

PARENT. Not much longer then.

CHILD. Why is it so cold?

PARENT. It's a fridge.

CHILD. But why?

PARENT. It's meat. And vegetables.

CHILD. Can we eat it?

PARENT. It's not ours.

CHILD. You said there'd be food.

PARENT. Not yet, but soon.

The truck comes to a stop. The voices of men talking, outside.

CHILD. It stopped.

PARENT. Shh.

CHILD. Can we go out, it's so cold.

PARENT. Shh. Be still. Remember.

CHILD. It's so cold.

PARENT. Remember, be still. Like wood. Like crates and boxes. They think we are boxes. Sacks. Vegetables. Be like a vegetable.

More men arrive.

CHILD. It's so cold.

PARENT. This is the stillest we must be in all our lives, baby. It's cold, yes, so be like ice. Think of ice. How heavy is a block of ice?

CHILD. I want to go home.

PARENT. Don't think about home.

CHILD. It was warm.

PARENT. No, ice. Cold. Still. Home? Okay, think of the river. The logs they sailed down the river. From our town to the next. Think of the logs. We are logs. Down the river. Rolling down. Going to a good place. Yes? Where logs turn back into trees. They'll fatten us up like cows. Rooms to sleep. Beds. No more sleeping head to feet. No more stinking feet.

CHILD. So cold.

PARENT. Shh.

The door of the container opens. A GUARDSMAN *enters, shining his torch. The light falls on the stowaways. A long silence. The* GUARDSMAN *approaches.*

GUARDSMAN. You.

PARENT. Please. Please if you understand. It is only my child and me. Where we're from there is no work, no food, there's gangs with guns come in the night. We're not too different, your people, mine. We do not understand each other, but we are not that different. Please. We have no papers, but please, mercy. Please let us. Please close the door. Turn off the light. Let us go.

The GUARDSMAN *approaches. Uses his foot to nudge* CHILD.

You saw no one. Please. It's just me and my child. Just the two of us. Not many. You will not feel us arrive. Please. We come to work. Make enough and go back. We don't mean to stay. Just to work and then leave. Please. I have a child.

The GUARDSMAN *looks at* PARENT *in the face. A long silence.*

You are a kind man. I can see it. Please.

The GUARDSMAN *slowly turns. Walks away. He steadies himself.*

GUARDSMAN (*on comms*). There's two bodies.

PARENT. A good man. A kind man. Thank you. Bless you. (*cradling* CHILD.) We will remember your face in our prayers. I pray for you, your children, that they will never in a generation, four generations, know the life we lead. Blessings on you.

GUARDSMAN. Fuck me.

Static from the comms.

(*On comms.*) Yeah just two.

PARENT. Baby, you'll wake up in a city of gold and glass.

PART THREE

1. Spaceship

Three hundred years later.

A space vessel. A garden on board. A body, FOUR, *lies curled amongst the plants, back facing the audience.* ONE, TWO, *and* THREE *are gathered nearby in heated discussion.*

ONE. There might be secretions. Glands, I've read, on the epidermis that secrete a kind of latex...

TWO. How did it get into the garden?

THREE. Is it alive?

TWO. Is the latex toxic?

THREE. Unconscious perhaps.

TWO. There is a real question of toxicity – the cabbages...

ONE. What?

TWO. The cabbages...

ONE. Shit it might contaminate the –

TWO. How did it even –

THREE. It looks so human...

ONE. A stow-away. Who found it?

THREE. Came up on the scans.

TWO. You don't have to look closely to see it's not human. They have bow-legs from lack of gravity.

THREE. I don't see any bow-legs.

ONE. The two of you shut up! Can't think. (*Pause.*) Do you smell something?

TWO. Smell...

ONE. Like gas, or burning…

TWO. Gas… It's the secretions.

THREE. Is it dead?

TWO. Do you think they release gases when they die? Maybe they decompose faster…

THREE. It's not dead.

ONE. It's not?

TWO. We should not be this close, we've been exposed.

THREE. I don't smell anything…

TWO. It's moving…

ONE. Shit, it's moving. Stand back!

THREE. It's…

    Pause.

    FOUR *groans.*

TWO. Do you hear that?

THREE. It's…

ONE. Oh shit.

THREE. It's…

TWO. What is that sound?

ONE. This is so awful.

THREE. We ought to help, she's clearly in pain!

ONE. She?

THREE. I see blood.

ONE. It's been shot.

THREE. Maybe we can suture the –

TWO. No!

THREE. Why?

ONE. I hear they're at war…

THREE. What?

ONE. With each other.

THREE. Listen, the wound is fresh.

ONE. They're at war with each other –

THREE. I'm gonna –

ONE. So – you're not listening

TWO. Shit.

ONE. So it can't remain on this ship, it'll become a diplomatic matter now. They'll see it as an act of war / we have to return it to the surface

TWO. Who will, exactly?

ONE. They've been known to be violent. Vicious.

TWO. That smell…

THREE. I just need to go get my kit, I can –

ONE. Wait, stop, we need to… think calmly.

THREE. It will take minutes.

ONE. No, the longer it stays here…

THREE. We can at least bandage…

TWO. He's right, this is *severely* out of our depth (*Brandishing a screen*.) Look here, it's a war between two religious sects… Between two ideological factions… Ethnic cleansing…

    FOUR *groans*.

ONE. Oh god.

THREE. I'm getting my kit.

ONE. Yeah alright. Alright.

TWO. No, stop.

    TWO *stops* THREE.

    It's genocide, it's war… it's not our place to interfere.

THREE. Who the fuck is going to know?

TWO. We don't interfere. (*To* ONE.) And besides. Toxicity. Cabbages. There's lives here. Ours, the others.

ONE. I know!

Pause.

We need to seek guidance from headquarters.

THREE. It would take hours to send a message.

ONE. It'll survive a few hours. Right?

THREE. What?

ONE. They're hardy. They're strong.

THREE. The wound is as big as your fist.

TWO. We should put it in a –

ONE. What? And

TWO. Send it back to the –

ONE. Yes, and

TWO. Out of our hands, into –

THREE. If I get my kit, I can suture the –

ONE. I can't risk a diplomatic –

TWO. It's already contaminating the air

ONE. And there's that too

THREE. Are you listening to yourself?

TWO. We ought to be masked, we ought

THREE. Are you listening to yourself?

ONE. It's about safety!

Beat.

ONE. It's about protocol! These are the things we live and die by. Alright?

TWO. I agree. It's unfortunate but.

THREE. I can suture the wound.

TWO. But there are too many unknowns.

THREE. I can…

ONE. We should…

TWO. Anything we do is…

ONE. Yes, a misstep. I agree. We should vote.

TWO. Vote. Yes.

THREE. No. I'm getting my kit.

ONE. If you go, I have no choice.

THREE. No choice

ONE. No choice but to… there are steps. I would have to

THREE. You're not seeing clearly.

ONE. You know I have to.

Silence. TWO *starts coughing.*

TWO. It's starting.

THREE. Stop that.

TWO. It must be.

ONE. We'll quarantine this place.

THREE. What, and just leave her –

ONE. Vote. All in favour?

THREE. Of *what*?

TWO. Non-interference?

ONE *and* TWO *raise their hands.*

ONE. That settles it. Let's go.

THREE. I…

ONE (*to* THREE). What you going to do then?

THREE. I…

Silence.

Can't we try talking to her at least?

ONE. What?

THREE. Just to say… I don't know…

> THREE *moves closer to* FOUR. THREE *leans in towards*
> FOUR, *who shrinks back, terrified.* THREE *puts a tentative*
> *arm on* FOUR's *shoulder. Moments pass.* THREE *gently*
> *embraces* FOUR.

THREE. She's warm.

TWO. You're compromised.

THREE. She smells so familiar.

TWO. We'll have to isolate them both.

THREE. Sweat. And fear, and loneliness.

2. Inside

A space beyond time, or at least history. THREE *and* FOUR *are*
holding each other.

The low, primordial noise of birds.

THREE. They've come
    The men
    Again
    Outside
    I heard them.
    The men.
    They'll find us

> *Silence.*

FOUR. Let them.
    how many times
    have they already
    found us.
    Us, already
    buried in rock

or sand
or fallen house
or burnt
or drowned
or drowned out
or poisoned
or driven away
or locked away
or lied to
or lied about
or desecrated
or defiled
or defeated
or disinterred
or done to
or done about
or…

THREE. That's enough.

Silence.

FOUR. And what can you say to that?

THREE. I dunno.

FOUR. What can you say to any of that?

Silence.

Perhaps the men draw closer.

THREE. Are you cold?
Are you hungry?

Beat.

Does it hurt?

Beat.

Let me see.

The End.

A Nick Hern Book

No Particular Order first published in Great Britain as a paperback original in 2022 by Nick Hern Books Limited, The Glasshouse, 49a Goldhawk Road, London W12 8QP, in association with Ellandar Productions and Theatre503

No Particular Order copyright © 2022 Joel Tan

Joel Tan has asserted his right to be identified as the author of this work

Cover image of Jules Chan; photography by Eivind Hansen, art direction by Louise Richardson

Designed and typeset by Nick Hern Books, London
Printed in Great Britain by Mimeo Ltd, Huntingdon, Cambridgeshire PE29 6XX

A CIP catalogue record for this book is available from the British Library

ISBN 978 1 83904 088 7

www.nickhernbooks.co.uk

facebook.com/nickhernbooks

twitter.com/nickhernbooks